THE BATTLE OF HASTINGS

T0309420

Contents

Written by Ben Hubbard

Collins

1 Why the Battle of Hastings is important

The year of 1066 began with bad news for England. King Edward lay ill on his deathbed. But there was worse news. Edward was childless. This meant there was no **heir** to succeed him. Who, then, would become the next king of England?

a re-enactment of the Battle of Hastings

This question led to the events of 1066. During this year, three **warlords** fought for control. Two kings died. England was attacked by Vikings and Normans. It ended with the Battle of Hastings and was the end of Anglo-Saxon England.

The Battle of Hastings is famous because the Anglo-Saxon leader, Harold, lost. But in many ways, it was a battle he could have won. So, what went wrong? Why did Harold lose Hastings? Read on to help investigate.

2 Anglo-Saxon England

In 1066, England was the envy of Europe. It was wealthy, powerful and well-protected. At the country's centre, was its king. Anglo-Saxon kings had ruled most of England for more than 500 years. These warrior kings defended their **realm** at the head of large armies. Without a king, the army and country were leaderless. This put the country's **borders** under serious risk of attack.

Much of what we know about the Battle of Hastings comes from the **Bayeux Tapestry**, made in the 1070s. Here, it shows King Edward.

When King Edward the Confessor died in January 1066 he had no heir, so it was unclear who should succeed him. There were four men who all had a claim to the throne. But only one of them could be crowned king. What do you think their claims were? What happened next?

King Edward's tomb lies in Westminster Abbey, London, UK.

3 Candidates for king

After King Edward died, four men thought they should be made king. Here, they explain why.

I'm Earl Harold Godwinson of Wessex, an Anglo-Saxon and the queen's brother. I was there when King Edward died. He said I should succeed him!

I'm Duke William of Normandy, King Edward's cousin. Edward and Harold Godwinson both promised I would be the next English king.

I'm Harald Hardrada, a Viking and King of Norway. I'm a descendant of King Harthacnut, who used to rule England. I should therefore be king!

I'm Edgar Atheling, Edward's great-nephew. Although I'm a blood relative, I'm only 14 years old. I probably won't be king!

Nobody had heard King Edward tell Harold that he should succeed him on his deathbed. However, the English nobles decided Harold would be a strong ruler who could defend England's shores. They crowned him King of England on 6th January, 1066. Was this fair? Who do you think should have been made king?

4 The wrath of William

William was furious when he heard Harold had been crowned king. William was a powerful warlord who ruled over Normandy, northern France. Edward had lived in Normandy for several years to escape a Viking invasion of England. According to William, this is when Edward promised to make him the next king of England.

William was born in 1028 in Falaise Castle, Normandy, France.

Later, Harold Godwinson stayed in Normandy too, after being shipwrecked there. According to William, Harold also promised William would be made the next king. But instead, Harold was now the king. William decided to take the English throne by force. He put together an army and a **fleet** of ships to invade England.

I will take what is owed to me!

5 The Norman army

William gathered an army of 7,000 **archers**, **foot soldiers** and knights on horseback to invade England. Each type of soldier played a vital part in the well-organised Norman army.

Archer

Archers wore light clothing so they could move quickly. They were armed with a longbow, or crossbow, and carried arrows in a quiver attached to their belts.

longbow

arrows

quiver (a case for holding arrows)

Foot soldier

Foot soldiers were armed with spears, swords and a club called a **mace**. For protection, they wore **chain mail** shirts and pointed helmets. They carried kite-shaped shields.

spear

shield

chain mail

lance

Knight

Mounted knights armed themselves with a lance, sword and mace. They wore a helmet and long chain mail shirt for protection. They also carried a shield.

6 The Anglo-Saxons

When King Harold heard about William's planned invasion, he marched an army to the Sussex coast, in the south of England. This is where William would land. King Harold's army was made up of full-time soldiers, called housecarls, and part-time soldiers, called the fyrd. The fyrd was made up of ordinary men, who only fought when they were needed.

axe

sword

Housecarl

Housecarls wore short chain mail shirts and pointed helmets. They carried round or kite-shaped shields. They fought with swords, axes, maces and spears.

Fyrd

The fyrd had more basic weapons and armour than the housecarls. Some had leather shirts, round shields, spears and daggers. But others had to make do with farmer's tools.

7 Vikings attack!

King Harold and his army waited weeks for William to arrive. But bad weather made crossing the English Channel too dangerous. In Normandy, William waited impatiently for good weather. The soldiers on both sides became restless.

In early September, King Harold received shocking news. A Viking army had landed in the north of England. It was led by King Harald Hardrada and King Harold's own brother, Tostig Godwinson. Now King Harold had a choice to make: march north and fight Harald, or stay put and wait for William. Why would this have been a difficult choice to make?

King Harold **exiled** his own brother! Now we are both out to overthrow him!

King Harald Hardrada

Tostig Godwinson

8 The Vikings

Harald Hardrada was a tough Viking king who had united all of Norway. Now, he wished to add England to his kingdom.

His army of over 10,000 Vikings sailed to England aboard 300 ships. The army landed in Yorkshire, north-east England, at the beginning of September.

The Vikings had been attacking England for over 300 years. In 1013, the Viking king Sweyn Forkbeard seized the English throne. It was then that the future king, Edward, fled to Normandy.

It was there, William said, that Edward had promised him the throne after he died.

The Vikings were warriors from the modern countries of Sweden, Norway and Denmark. They attacked many European countries in their **longships**.

9 King Harold marches

After landing, Harald marched his Viking army towards the city of York, north England. The Anglo-Saxon Northern Earls rode out with their soldiers to meet Harald. They fought a battle at a place called Fulford. But the Vikings easily defeated the Anglo-Saxons. Now, King Harold had little choice but to march quickly north and fight the Vikings.

The Vikings are killing Anglo-Saxons. I must stop them!

Viking warriors

Vikings were armed with axes, spears, swords, and bows and arrows. They protected themselves with iron helmets, chain mail shirts and round shields. By locking their shields together, the Vikings formed a "shield wall" during battle. This was also a **tactic** the Anglo-Saxons used.

a modern re-enactment of a Viking shield wall

10 The Battle of Stamford Bridge

To fight the Vikings, King Harold's army marched over 320 kilometres in just seven days.

Normally, the journey took two weeks! Many men joined King Harold as he marched. By the time he reached Yorkshire, north England on 25th September, King Harold's army had 15,000 men.

The speed and size of King Harold's army caught the Vikings by surprise. They were camped at a place called Stamford Bridge, when King Harold's army arrived. Many Vikings did not even have their armour with them. Despite fighting bravely, the Vikings were defeated. Harald Hardrada and Tostig were killed.

In this Battle of Stamford Bridge painting from 1870, Harald is shown with an arrow in his neck.

21

11 Invasion!

King Harold had won a great victory at the Battle of Stamford Bridge. The Vikings would never again attack England. But as King Harold and his men celebrated, there was terrible news. William had landed his army at Pevensey, Sussex, south-east England on 28th September.

William lands in England.

King Harold had little choice but to turn his army around and march to fight William. But King Harold's army was tired after the march north and the Battle of Stamford Bridge. Some soldiers were dead. Others had left. King Harold had to march south with a much smaller army.

Lots of my friends went back to work their fields rather than fight William.

SCOTLAND

- ⛵---- Harald's crossing of the North Sea
- 🚶---- Harold's march north from London
- ⛵---- William's crossing from France
- ✗ Battle site

Present day countries shown

North
Sea

NORTHERN
IRELAND

Isle of Man

Irish Sea

IRELAND

York   *Stamford*
        ✗ *Bridge*
    ✗
Fulford

ENGLAND   🚶

WALES

London

This map shows
the events of 1066.

✗ *Battle*

Pevensey   *Hastings*
        ⛵

English Channel

St-Valery-sur-Somme

Channel Islands

FRANCE

23

12 March to Hastings

By 8th October, King Harold had reached London on his march south. He paused there to gather more men and speak to his advisors. These included his mother and brother. Both wanted King Harold to wait until he had more men before facing William. Should he have listened to them?

Meanwhile, William had built a wooden castle in Hastings, Sussex, south-east England. His men were **raiding** villages and burning homes. Hearing these reports angered King Harold. Even if his army was not at full strength, he decided to march to Hastings at once.

King Harold, wait in London for reinforcements. Let your brother Gyrth fight William in the meantime.

Gytha Godwinson, mother of King Harold

a re-enactment of the Anglo-Saxon
soldiers marching south

13 Battle lines

The Battle of Hastings did not actually take place
in Hastings. Instead, it was fought 12 kilometres away
on a hill called Senlac. At dawn, on 14th October,
King Harold's army formed a line along the top of
the hill. Banners fluttered in the morning breeze,
as 7,000 Anglo-Saxon soldiers looked down on
the Norman army.

People re-enacting
the Battle of Hastings
get into position.

Looking up from the bottom of the hill was William's army. It had around 7,000 men. Having to fight uphill put William at a disadvantage. However, he hoped his mighty knights and archers would win the day for him.

Our horses have been trained to charge at the enemy. The Anglo-Saxons don't even use their horses in battle! They just ride them to the battleground.

14 Into battle!

At about 9 o'clock in the morning, the battle began.
King Harold ordered the men at the front of his line
to lock their shields together to form a shield wall.
He shouted that the wall must hold, no matter what.

Anglo-Saxon battle lines

Below, William formed his army into three lines: archers, foot soldiers and knights. He then ordered his archers to step forward and fire at the Anglo-Saxons. This had little effect. Because the archers were firing uphill, many arrows bounced off the Anglo-Saxon shields.

Norman battle lines

15 Holding the shield wall

To try and break King Harold's shield wall, William ordered his foot soldiers and knights to attack.
As the Normans charged, the Anglo-Saxons launched things at them: spears, axes and even rocks.
Then the Normans crashed against the shield wall. But the wall held strong. The Anglo-Saxons thrust their swords and spears at the Normans through gaps in the wall.

Suddenly, somebody shouted that William was dead! In a panic, the Normans on the left of their line stopped attacking and ran down the hill.
Some Anglo-Saxons chased them.

It was like hitting a stone wall.
There was no way through.

The Normans try and break through
the Anglo-Saxon shield wall,
in this re-enactment.

31

16 Anglo-Saxon defeat

King Harold despaired when he saw his men running after the Normans. Now there was a big hole in his army's shield wall. He ordered his soldiers to fill the gap and form a new wall. The Anglo-Saxons who had run after the Normans were now on their own.

Norman knights hunted down the Anglo-Saxons who broke **ranks**.

Meanwhile, the rumour about William's death proved to be false. To stop his men fleeing, William took off his helmet and rode across the battlefield to prove that he was alive. He then ordered his knights to surround and kill the Anglo-Saxons who had broken ranks. All King Harold could do was stand and watch.

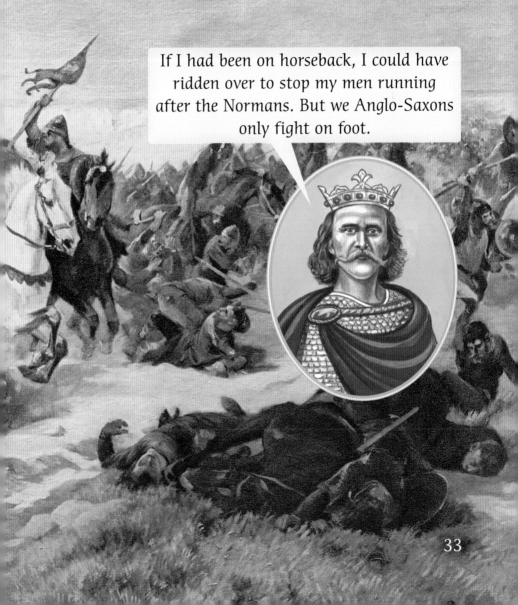

If I had been on horseback, I could have ridden over to stop my men running after the Normans. But we Anglo-Saxons only fight on foot.

17 Fight and flight

Seeing the Anglo-Saxons run after the fleeing Normans gave William an idea. If his men attacked and then pretended to retreat, the Anglo-Saxons might chase them again. This would create new holes in the shield wall.

If I break through that shield wall, then I can win this battle.

On the Bayeux Tapestry, the Anglo-Saxons try to hold against the Norman knights.

From midday, William used this new tactic. It began to have results. When the Anglo-Saxons chased the Normans, William's knights rode in and killed the exposed soldiers. Slowly, King Harold's army began to thin out. But they were not yet beaten.

18 Death and defeat

By the late afternoon, William was tiring the Anglo-Saxons out. He ordered his archers to form a line behind his soldiers attacking the shield wall. This time, he had the archers fire up into the air, so their arrows would rain down on the Anglo-Saxons.

Norman archers prepare to fire, in this re-enactment.

Suddenly, a shout went up from the Anglo-Saxons. King Harold had been killed. With their king dead, the army fell apart. The Normans stormed the hill and killed anyone who could not run from them. By dusk, the battle was lost. William would be the new king of England.

I heard that King Harold was killed by an arrow to the eye. Others said a Norman **death squad** killed him.

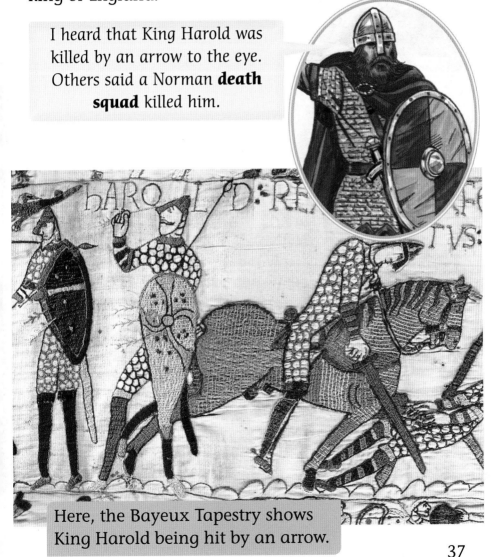

Here, the Bayeux Tapestry shows King Harold being hit by an arrow.

19 Why did King Harold lose Hastings?

Thousands of Anglo-Saxons died at the Battle of Hastings, including King Harold. He would be England's last Anglo-Saxon king. Now, the country would experience great change and suffering under a new Norman king. Could this have been avoided? What were the reasons King Harold lost the Battle of Hastings?

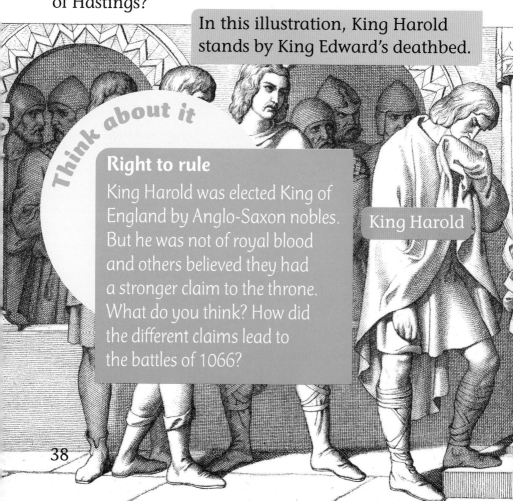

In this illustration, King Harold stands by King Edward's deathbed.

King Harold

Think about it

Right to rule

King Harold was elected King of England by Anglo-Saxon nobles. But he was not of royal blood and others believed they had a stronger claim to the throne. What do you think? How did the different claims lead to the battles of 1066?

Fighting on two fronts

Harald Hardrada's attack in the north exhausted and weakened King Harold's army. Did this change how King Harold's men fought at the Battle of Hastings? Could King Harold have won if his army was fresher?

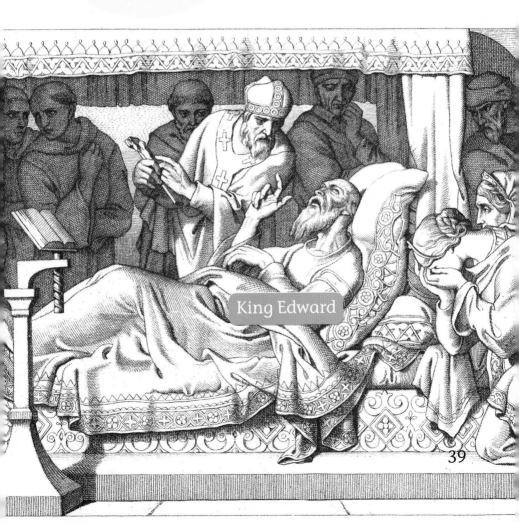

King Edward

39

A wooden archer marks the Battle of Hastings battlefield. An abbey was built on the spot where King Harold was killed.

Bad decisions?

King Harold's mother and brother pleaded with him to wait in London for reinforcements. But he didn't listen. Could he have waited for reinforcements? Or did he have to stop William attacking his people? How did this affect the Battle of Hastings?

No archers or knights

Anglo-Saxon armies travelled on horseback but did not ride them into battle. King Harold also had few archers compared to the Normans. What advantages did William's knights and archers give him on the battlefield? What if King Harold had used more of these soldiers?

Lack of discipline

After the Battle of Stamford Bridge, King Harold was forced to rely on his less disciplined fyrd soldiers against William. Many of these broke the shield wall and chased the Normans. Was this when the battle began to go against King Harold? Could he have stopped them breaking the shield wall? What if he had been on horseback?

20 After Hastings

William crowned himself King of England in Westminster Abbey on Christmas Day 1066. However, many Anglo-Saxon nobles **rebelled** against their new leader. William quickly killed these rebels. He then built castles all over the country and installed Norman nobles to rule over the local people. He soon gaineda reputation for being a cruel and brutal king.

William began building the Tower of London in 1066. It still stands today.

William would be remembered as "the **conqueror**". However, the Norman conquest of England only lasted for 50 years. Afterwards, a new dynasty of French kings, called the Plantagenets, took over. Over time, French and Anglo-Saxon culture and customs merged to form the modern country of the United Kingdom of today.

Glossary

archers soldiers who fight with a bow and arrow

Bayeux Tapestry a 70-metre long piece of cloth embroidered to show the events surrounding the Battle of Hastings

borders invisible lines that separate two countries

chain mail an armour shirt of small metal rings linked together

conqueror a person who invades a place by force

fleet a group of ships

foot soldiers soldiers who fight on foot, as opposed to on horseback

heir the person who will succeed the monarch, usually their son or daughter

longship a long, narrow boat used by Vikings

mace a heavy spiked club

raiding making a surprise attack, usually on a village or town

ranks a line of soldiers in battle

realm a kingdom

rebelled rose up against a leader

tactic a plan of action to achieve a result

warlords military commanders who live for battle

Index

Harold's moments in history

This timeline shows some of the key moments in 1066 that led to King Harold's defeat. Which moments do you think most contributed to his downfall? Why, in the end, did King Harold lose Hastings?

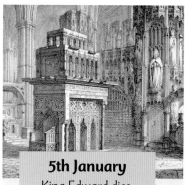

5th January
King Edward dies. There are four candidates who all want to replace him.

25th September
King Harold marches his army 320 kilometres to fight Harald at Stamford Bridge.

8th September
Harald Hardrada lands his Viking army in the north of England.

8th October
On his march south
to meet William,
King Harold pauses
in London. Here, he
receives advice.

28th September
William lands in
Sussex at the head
of a large army.
His army starts raiding
English villages.

14th October
During the Battle of
Hastings, King Harold's
men break their
shield wall.

Ideas for reading

Written by Christine Whitney
Primary Literacy Consultant

Reading objectives:
- be introduced to non-fiction books that are structured in different ways
- listen to, discuss and express views about non-fiction
- retrieve and record information from non-fiction
- discuss and clarify the meanings of words

Spoken language objectives:
- participate in discussion
- speculate, hypothesise, imagine and explore ideas through talk
- ask relevant questions

Curriculum links: History: Develop an awareness of the past; Writing: Write for different purposes

Word count: 2967

Interest words: wrath, heir, realm, shield wall, conqueror

Resources: paper, pencils and crayons, access to the internet, map of England

Build a context for reading

- Ask children to name the present Queen of England. Ask for a volunteer to name any other King or Queen of England.
- Ask children to give today's date. Note the year. Now ask them to travel back over 1000 years to 1066. Explain that this is the year of a famous battle called The Battle of Hastings. Use a map of England to show both Hastings and York. Ask children to find where their nearest town is on the map.
- Show the book cover to them and read the title, *The Battle of Hastings*. Challenge children to make predictions about why the battle may have been lost.

Understand and apply reading strategies

- Read together up to the end of Chapter 3. Ask children to summarise why there was a problem when King Edward died. Support children to use the word *heir* in their answer.